P9-CBU-084

EXPLORING COUNTRIES

Cambodia

by Walter Simmons

BELLWETHER MEDIA • MINNEAPOLIS, MN

Note to Librarians, Teachers, and Parents:

Blastoff! Readers are carefully developed by literacy experts and combine standards-based content with developmentally appropriate text.

Level 1 provides the most support through repetition of high-frequency words, light text, predictable sentence patterns, and strong visual support.

Level 2 offers early readers a bit more challenge through varied simple sentences, increased text load, and less repetition of high-frequency words.

Level 3 advances early-fluent readers toward fluency through increased text and concept load, less reliance on visuals, longer sentences, and more literary language.

Level 4 builds reading stamina by providing more text per page, increased use of punctuation, greater variation in sentence patterns, and increasingly challenging vocabulary.

Level 5 encourages children to move from "learning to read" to "reading to learn" by providing even more text, varied writing styles, and less familiar topics.

Whichever book is right for your reader, Blastoff! Readers are the perfect books to build confidence and encourage a love of reading that will last a lifetime!

This edition first published in 2012 by Bellwether Media, Inc.

No part of this publication may be reproduced in whole or in part without written permission of the publisher. For information regarding permission, write to Bellwether Media, Inc., Attention: Permissions Department, 5357 Penn Avenue South, Minneapolis, MN 55419.

Library of Congress Cataloging-in-Publication Data

Simmons, Walter (Walter G.)
 Cambodia / by Walter Simmons.
    p. cm. – (Blastoff! readers) (Exploring countries)
Includes bibliographical references and index.
 Summary: "Developed by literacy experts for students in grades three through seven, this book introduces young readers to the geography and culture of Cambodia"–Provided by publisher.
 ISBN 978-1-60014-726-5 (hardcover : alk. paper)
 1. Cambodia–Juvenile literature. I. Title. II. Series: Blastoff! readers. III. Series: Exploring countries.
DS554.3.S56 2012
959.6–dc23   2011029471

Text copyright © 2012 by Bellwether Media, Inc. BLASTOFF! READERS and associated logos are trademarks and/or registered trademarks of Bellwether Media, Inc. SCHOLASTIC, CHILDREN'S PRESS, and associated logos are trademarks and/or registered trademarks of Scholastic Inc.

Printed in the United States of America, North Mankato, MN.

010112   1203

Contents

Where Is Cambodia?   4
The Land   6
The Tonle Sap   8
Wildlife   10
The People   12
Daily Life   14
Going to School   16
Working   18
Playing   20
Food   22
Holidays   24
Angkor Wat   26
Fast Facts   28
Glossary   30
To Learn More   31
Index   32

Laos

Thailand

Cambodia

Tonle Sap

Mekong River

Phnom Penh

Gulf of Thailand

Did you know?

At one time, the Khmer Empire ruled over the lands of Cambodia, Laos, Thailand, and Vietnam. The empire fell apart in the 1400s.

Vietnam

Cambodia is a country in Southeast Asia that covers 69,898 square miles (181,035 square kilometers). It shares a long northwestern border with Thailand. In the east, it has a lengthy border with Vietnam. Cambodia and Laos share a smaller border in the north. Cambodia's southwestern coast meets the **Gulf** of Thailand. The Mekong River flows into Cambodia from Laos and then into Vietnam. Phnom Penh, the capital of Cambodia, lies on the banks of this mighty river.

N
W   E
S

Cambodia is a land of tropical forests, small mountain ranges, and rolling plains. Most of the country's people live in a low-lying **basin** that covers the central and eastern half of the country. The Mekong River flows through the eastern part of this basin.

The Cardamom Mountains rise in the southwest. They include Phnom Aural, a peak that reaches a height of 5,949 feet (1,813 meters). It is the highest point in Cambodia. To the southeast rise the Elephant Mountains. The Dangrek Mountains mark part of the border between Cambodia and Thailand. In the northeast, near the border with Laos, rise the Northeastern Highlands. Dense tropical forests cover these steep hills.

fun fact

For hundreds of years, Cambodians have used ferries to cross the Mekong River. In 2001, a bridge was built to span the river.

Did you know?

Many Cambodians earn a living fishing the Tonle Sap. Thousands of fishing families live in floating homes along the lakeshore.

The Tonle Sap is a lake that covers a plain in central Cambodia. During most of the year, the Tonle Sap is only about 3 feet (1 meter) deep. The lake narrows into a river, which flows south and joins the Mekong. The two rivers meet just north of Phnom Penh.

When **monsoon season** comes, heavy rains fall in Cambodia. The Mekong River floods and the Tonle Sap River reverses course. High waters move north into the lake. At this time of year, the lake can reach a depth of 45 feet (14 meters). The lake floods to cover four times as much land!

Cambodia is home to a variety of animals. Tigers, leopards, bears, boars, and wild dogs all roam the forests of the Cardamom Mountains. This range is also home to a small number of wild elephants. Above the forest floor, gibbons and macaques rest and find food in the trees. On the ground below, cobras, kraits, and other deadly snakes slither in search of prey.

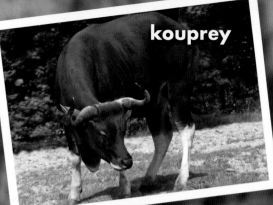

kouprey

heron

gibbon

Herons, egrets, pelicans, and hornbills gather near coastal areas and rivers. In the Gulf of Thailand, eels, crabs, and tropical fish find homes on the sea floor. They watch out for sharks, dolphins, and other ocean predators.

More than 14 million people live in Cambodia. Many centuries ago, the Khmer **migrated** to Cambodia from the north. Today this is the largest people group in the country. Khmer is also the official language of Cambodia. Chinese, Vietnamese, and Laotians also live in the country. The Cham people speak their own language and follow **Islam**. They live north of Phnom Penh in central Cambodia.

Several **hill tribes** live in the northeast. Many of their small villages have no roads or electricity. The hill tribes have their own customs and languages. They live in small houses made of bamboo and palm wood.

Speak Khmer!

Khmer is written in script. However, Khmer words can be written in English to help you read them out loud.

English	Khmer	How to say it
hello	sour sdey	so ur-sa dei
good-bye	lear heouy	lea hoy
yes (male)	jas	jahs
yes (female)	bat	bah
no	te	te-ah
please	suom	sue-um
thank you	ar kun	are kun
friend	met pheak	meht feek

In Cambodia's busy and crowded cities, most people get around on motorbikes, bicycles, or buses. At street markets, they can buy **poultry**, nuts, fried insects, and baskets of fruit. Many restaurants have sidewalk tables and are open late. In the evening, people visit friends and family.

In the countryside, people work in the fields to plant and harvest crops. Some use trucks to get around, but many use carts pulled by **oxen**. They buy goods in village markets or small shops. Many houses in the countryside are built on **stilts** so they do not flood during monsoon season.

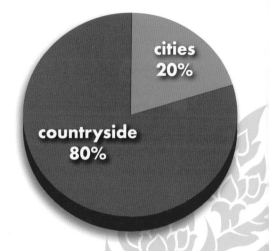

Where People Live in Cambodia

cities 20%

countryside 80%

15

In Cambodia, children begin school at the age of 6. Primary school lasts six years. Some kids continue with lower secondary school, which lasts for three years. Upper secondary school goes through grade twelve. Those who complete secondary school can move on to universities.

Although education is free in Cambodia, many children do not attend school. Some work to support their families. Those who can attend must deal with crowded classrooms and a limited number of books and supplies.

Did you know?

Some boys in Cambodia spend a year as a Buddhist monk. They live in a monastery and study Buddhism with older teachers.

Where People Work in Cambodia

farming 58%

manufacturing 16%

services 26%

Did you know?

Fishing is the most important job along the Mekong River and on the Tonle Sap. Fishers use large nets to snare hundreds of fish.

Many Cambodians farm the land. Rice is the country's **staple crop**. Farmers also grow sweet potatoes, cashews, sugarcane, and many other crops. Some raise pigs, cattle, and poultry. Cambodia **exports** timber from its tropical forests. Cambodian miners dig up sapphires, rubies, and other gemstones.

In the cities, factory workers make clothing, shoes, and household goods. Many city workers hold **service jobs** in banks, hospitals, and stores. They also work in hotels, restaurants, and other places that serve **tourists** who come to Cambodia.

sey

In their free time, Cambodians enjoy meeting their friends over a meal. Young people visit Internet cafés, where they can go online to play video games. On the street, crowds often watch small groups play a game of *sey*. Players keep a small ball in the air by using just their feet and legs.

Soccer is the country's most popular team sport. Everyone follows the matches of the national team, the Angkor Warriors. Tennis and badminton are popular individual sports. Cambodians also enjoy *pradel serey*, or kickboxing. Opponents can use punches and kicks to knock each other down. Traditional music is played during matches.

pradel serey

Did you know?

Fried insects are a popular snack in Cambodia. At street markets, Cambodians buy crunchy spiders, crickets, grasshoppers, and beetles to enjoy as treats!

Fish and rice are eaten daily in Cambodia. Rice soup with fish sauce is a favorite at any time of day. A common meal throughout the country is rice with *prahoc*, a spicy paste made from fish. *Amok* is a dish of fish, coconut milk, and turmeric, a popular herb. These ingredients are wrapped in banana leaves and then cooked.

Cambodians enjoy mangoes, pineapples, bananas, and **durians**. The durian has a bad smell, but it tastes sweet. A special treat is sweet coconut milk poured over sticky rice and mango slices. *Sankhya lapov* is another popular dessert. A slice of pumpkin is stuffed with coconut custard, then baked in an oven.

amok

durian

Independence Day

Cambodians celebrate many holidays. The Khmer New Year falls in April. People light candles, burn **incense**, and remember their **ancestors**. In April or May, Cambodians celebrate the birthday of Gautama Buddha, the founder of **Buddhism**. The Feast of the Ancestors usually takes place in September. Cambodians believe the ghosts of their ancestors visit them at **pagodas** during this time.

Independence Day falls on November 9. This marks the nation's independence from France. On January 7, Cambodia holds Victory Day. This holiday celebrates the end of the **Khmer Rouge**. During the late 1970s, many Cambodians died under this brutal **regime**.

dragon boat

Angkor Wat is the largest religious structure in the world. Located in northern Cambodia, it was built by a Cambodian ruler over 800 years ago. It was the capital of the Khmer Empire for 600 years. *Angkor Wat* means "city temple" in Khmer. A 2.2-mile (3.6-kilometer) wall surrounds the temple complex, and a **moat** surrounds the wall.

Angkor Wat was a **Hindu** temple before it became a place where Buddhists worship. Artists have carved thousands of **relief** sculptures in the walls around the temple. The sculptures show images significant to these two religions. Tourists visit Angkor Wat to see an important part of Cambodian history. Cambodians take great pride in Angkor Wat and its place in their culture, history, and tradition.

Fast Facts About Cambodia

Cambodia's Flag

The flag of Cambodia has two horizontal stripes of blue and a central band of red. A white image of Angkor Wat lies in the center. It is the only national flag to feature a building. Cambodia adopted this design after it won independence in 1948.

Official Name: Kingdom of Cambodia

Area: 69,898 square miles (181,035 square kilometers); Cambodia is the 90th largest country in the world.

Capital City:	Phnom Penh
Important Cities:	Siem Reap, Battambang, Sihanoukville
Population:	14,701,717 (July 2011)
Official Language:	Khmer
National Holiday:	Independence Day (November 9)
Religions:	Buddhist (96.4%), Muslim (2.1%), Other (1.5%)
Major Industries:	farming, fishing, logging, manufacturing, mining, services, tourism
Natural Resources:	fish, timber, gemstones, iron ore, hydropower, manganese, natural gas, oil
Manufactured Products:	clothing, cement, food products, rubber, chemicals, mechanical equipment
Farm Products:	rice, sugarcane, cassava, sweet potatoes, bananas, corn, beans, cashews, tapioca, soybeans, cattle, pigs, poultry
Unit of Money:	Cambodian riel; the riel is divided into 100 sen.

Glossary

ancestors—relatives who lived long ago

basin—an area of land surrounding a river; the water from a basin drains into a river.

Buddhism—a religion that follows the teachings of Buddha; Buddhists value nonviolence, compassion, and self-control.

durians—strong-smelling fruits; durians smell bad but have a very sweet taste.

exports—sells and sends to another country

gulf—part of an ocean that extends into land

hill tribes—groups of people that live in remote, mountainous areas of Cambodia

Hindu—relating to Hinduism; Hinduism is the dominant religion in India.

incense—a substance that produces a pleasant smell when burned

Islam—a religion that follows the teachings of the Prophet Muhammad

Khmer Rouge—a harsh government that ruled Cambodia in the 1970s

migrated—moved from one country or region to another, often with the seasons

moat—a deep, wide ditch filled with water; moats are built around buildings to protect them from attack.

monsoon season—the time of year when Cambodia receives a lot of rain; monsoon season falls between May and October.

oxen—domesticated bulls used to do work

pagodas—towers in eastern Asian countries that are several stories high; pagodas are built as temples or memorials to dead relatives.

poultry—birds raised for their eggs or meat

regime—a government or political party that rules a country; the Khmer Rouge was a brutal regime that ruled Cambodia in the late 1970s.

relief—a kind of sculpture in which figures are carved out of a flat surface

service jobs—jobs that perform tasks for people or businesses

staple crop—a common food crop that people eat often; rice is the staple crop of Cambodia.

stilts—posts that hold a building above ground

tourists—people who are visiting a country

To Learn More

AT THE LIBRARY
Candee, Helen Churchill. *Angkor the Magnificent: Wonder City of Ancient Cambodia*. Holmes Beach, Fla.: DatAsia, 2011.

Kras, Sara Louise. *Cambodia*. New York, N.Y.: Children's Press, 2005.

Lord, Michelle. *A Song for Cambodia*. New York, N.Y.: Lee & Low Books, 2008.

ON THE WEB

Learning more about Cambodia is as easy as 1, 2, 3.

1. Go to www.factsurfer.com.

2. Enter "Cambodia" into the search box.

3. Click the "Surf" button and you will see a list of related Web sites.

With factsurfer.com, finding more information is just a click away.

Index

activities, 20
Angkor Wat, 26-27
Buddhism, 17, 24, 27
capital (see Phnom Penh)
Cardamom Mountains, 6, 10
daily life, 14-15
education, 16-17
Feast of the Ancestors, 24
food, 22-23
Gulf of Thailand, 4, 5, 11
Hinduism, 27
holidays, 24-25
housing, 8, 13, 15
Independence Day, 24
Islam, 13
Khmer Empire, 4, 26
Khmer Rouge, 24
landscape, 6-9
languages, 13
location, 4-5
Mekong River, 4, 5, 6, 8,
    9, 18
monsoon season, 9, 15
peoples, 12-13
Phnom Aural, 6
Phnom Penh, 4, 5, 8, 13
sports, 21
Tonle Sap, 8-9, 18
transportation, 14, 15
Victory Day, 24

Water and Moon Festival, 25
wildlife, 10-11
working, 8, 15, 18-19